ABOUT WAYNE HARRISON

- Ex-Professional Player with Blackpool; England and Oulu Palloseura; Finland
- Represented Great Britain in the World Student Games in Mexico
- Bachelors of Arts in Sports Psychology
- UEFA 'A' License 1996
- NSCAA Premier Diploma holder
- Author of 14 Coaching Books and 4 DVD's
- DOC for Al Ain Soccer Club; United Arab Emirates; Middle East; 7 Youth National Championships in 2 years at Professional level
- Proponent of Soccer Awareness One Touch Developmental Training
- Owner Soccer Awareness Developmental Training programs

The Coconut Game - Dribbling With the Ball

Objective: To Improve player's technique, accuracy and weight of passing.

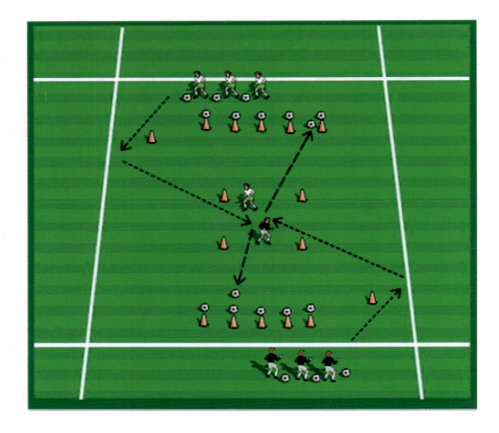

Organization
- Area: 15 x 10
- 2 Teams of 4-6 Players
- Each Team has 5 small discs with 5 soccer balls on top of them. A box in the middle marked out by 4 cones 5 x 5. A cone is placed 10 yards at the side of each Team.
- Players have to dribble the ball around the cone, and take the ball into the box.
- Players then have to pass the ball and attempt to knock the balls of the cones. The team that knocks all the balls of the cones is the winning team.

Key Coaching Points:
- Passing with the inside of the Foot, Use Both Feet.
- Lock Ankles
- Pass through the Middle part of the Soccer Ball,
- Correct Weight and Speed of Pass
- Have good accuracy on the Pass

Coconut Game 2 - Wall Passing / Give and Go's

Objective: To Improve player's technique, accuracy and weight of passing.

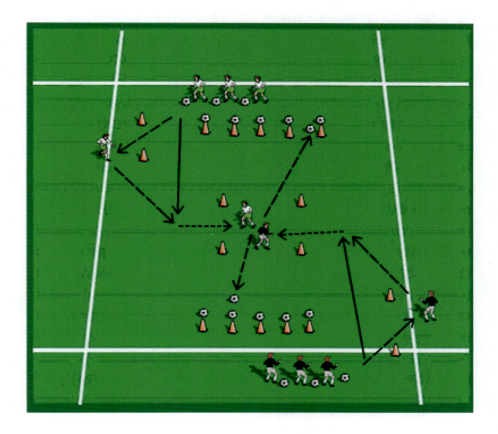

Organization
- Area: 15 x 10
- 2 Teams of 4-6 Players
- Each Team has 5 small discs with 5 soccer balls on top of them. A box in the middle marked out by 4 cones 5 x 5
- A cone is placed 10 yards at the side of each Team.
- Players start by passing between cones into Coach / Player. Player then runs forward and receives a pass back from Coach / Player.
- (Wall Pass)
- Player then takes the ball into box and tries to knock balls off cones. First team that knocks all the balls of the cones is the winning team.
- Start with 2 touches, Control and Pass
- Communication

Improving Touch On the Ball

Individual Ball Skills

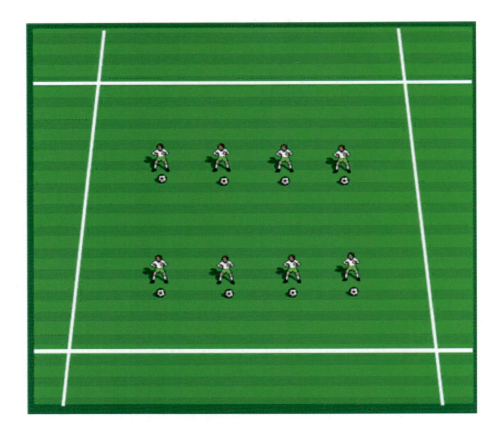

Using different techniques to control the ball.

1. Simple juggling of the ball to improve foot control, how many times can they keep it up with BOTH feet? Make it a competition between the players.
2. Using the inside and the outside of the feet and moving side to side. Move the ball with the inside of the foot then the outside to bring it back but with the same foot. Use a cutting motion.
3. Inside and outside of the foot, roll the ball to the outside (on top of the ball contact), cut it back with the inside and roll the ball to the inside and cut it back with the outside of the foot.

Moving a yard or so either side, back and forth maintaining control of the ball, this is great for acquiring a good touch on the ball and improving co-ordination.

Remind them to keep their head up not just looking at the ball all the time, even ask them to look around the area when they are doing this or the coach can hold up so many fingers and they have to call the number out as they work.

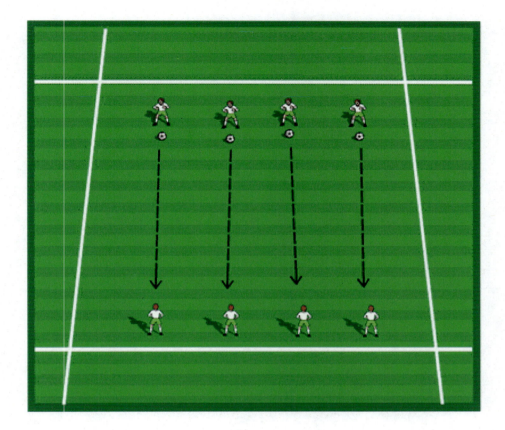

Simple passing in two's back and forth, first two touches, then one touch where possible. Coach can dictate the distance between them.

Ask the players to look into "each others eyes" as they pass and NOT at the ball to see if they can keep possession between them.

This will be difficult at first but it helps to teach them to look up and not down at the ball during games and hence helping their "Awareness" development as players.

They should be able to see their ball in the "peripheral vision".

Using both feet to pass the ball.

Competitive: Count how many passes they can get in between them during a given time.

Controlling Techniques in Two's

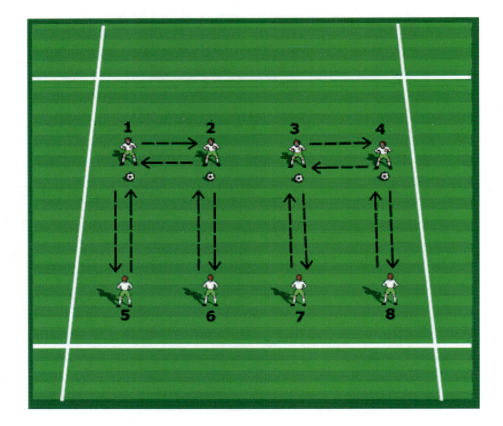

Working in pairs, once the task has been performed have the end players switch with each other, (1) and (2) switch for example. Servers stay in the same position and do 10 each then change.

Techniques to practice can be:

1. Throw to feet to control in one touch and pass back (right and left)
2. Throw to chest to chest down and pass back one touch on the half volley
3. Throw to thigh to control and pass back one touch on the half volley
4. Throw to head to head straight back (defensive or attacking headers)
5. Throw to head to cushion down and pass back on the half volley one touch
6. Throw to both feet alternatively so they have to control and pass with both feet
7. Throw and control with various parts of the body and volley the ball back.
8. Combinations, chest, thigh, then pass one touch on the half volley.
9. Throw to the ground, one bounce to the player who half volleys it back on the next bounce into their teammates hands, softly and under control.

Use your imagination to practice other techniques, vary the distances between the players and so on.

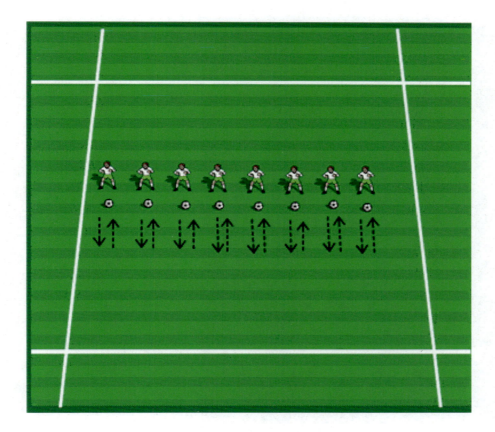

1. Players standing in the same position have to use one foot to "pull" the ball back with the "sole" of the foot and "push" the ball forward with the "laces" of the same foot.

2. These are simple repetitions to repeat constantly to get a feel for the ball and to improve ball control and first touch and also co-ordination.

3. For younger players doing it for the first time they need to do this at walking pace. Drag back with the sole, push forward with the laces. Then do the same routine with the other foot.

4. Then comment on the foot without the ball, the players will be flat footed so they need to be bouncing on the other foot as they do the exercise. Demonstrate the difference between receiving a pass flat footed and on their toes and lively.

5. Now they need to do the movement with their heads up, looking around not down at the ball all the time to develop awareness, ask questions of the players as to why they need to do this. Same idea but drag back with the sole push forward with the side of the foot not the laces.

Improving Touch On the Ball

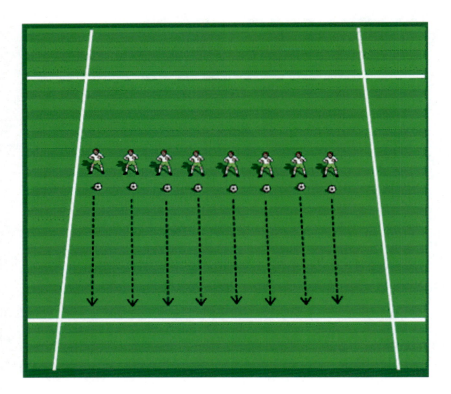

Coaching Points:
1. Good balance
2. High Concentration on the technique
3. On your toes not flat footed
4. Head Up whilst performing the task for Peripheral Awareness

Do it in a circle facing North, South, East and West on the call of the coach or have for example ten pulls with the sole and pushes with the laces movements at each direction. Quarter turns on each call going around in a circle.

Competitive: between the players to see who can do them the quickest but under total control and with correct technique.

On the coaches signal (AS SHOWN ABOVE) they now move up and down the field tapping the ball from foot to foot. After four taps they pull the ball back with the sole and push it out with the laces and move up field. Once they get to the other end they turn back and repeat the exercise, this gives them lots of good touches on the ball to improve their control.

Progressions:

1. Up and down the field with the right foot
2. Same with the left foot
3. Alternate feet up and down
4. The same routine but with the side of the foot not the laces.

Build some combinations into these routines, introducing turns and moves.

Move forward doing 20 push / pulls then do a step over turn and repeat with 20 back to where you started.

Individual Dribbling Skills - Working On Specific Dribbling Moves: The Technical Development of Dribbling: The Matthews, Rivelino, Double Touch and The Scissors

Shadow Dribbling

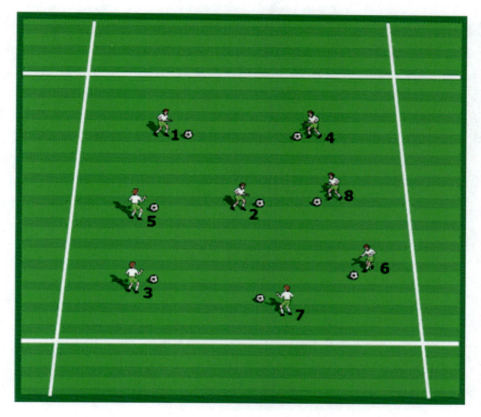

1. Practicing for example the Matthews shadow dribble. The balls are static and players address a ball and do the dribble without touching the ball.

2. This is a great introduction to the skill to gain success easily.

3. Players jog around and do the specified shadow dribbling skill at each ball.

4. They get lots of opportunities to practice the skill in a very relaxed non competitive environment. Do each of the specified dribbles this way.

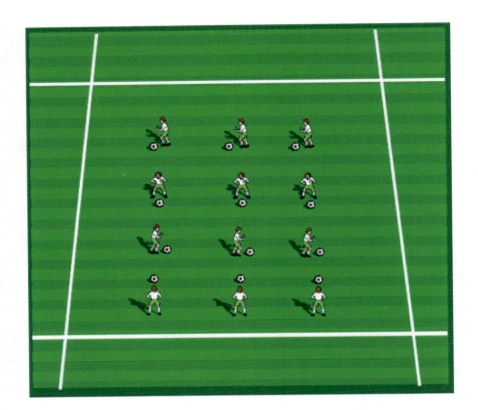

Coaching Points:

1. Technical dribbling skills but focusing on one at a time to master it. The skill is broken down in phases for ease of teaching.
2. Non competitive dribbling initially so players are able to relax when practicing
3. Observation: Constant reminders of players need to look around and not just down at the ball (awareness in possession of the ball).

Coaches can use these or any other moves that they like, these are good ones that I have included as examples but by all means try a new one if you are so inclined. When players receive the ball and are aware in advance that there is no option to pass and they may need to dribble to get out of trouble or to beat a player to get a shot at goal, then we need to players to have the ability to do this. This is again building up to the awareness concept being engrained in the player's makeup. Hence we are trying to teach the players some basic dribbles and tricks on the ball that they can use once they have identified the best option next is to dribble with the ball in this particular situation.

The above set up is an example of the progressive movement of one group of players. You can have 4 groups set up this way. Practicing a dribble from bottom to top, this is the routine working around the ball four times on the call of the coach each time facing another 45 degrees around the ball. Do the moves then stop and wait for the next call. All players work in unison. This is the total movement of one line of players but work with two lines opposite each other to help the development of the clinic (see over). Move around the ball both ways so players work on both sides with both feet. You get four dribbles / moves per rotation. Do it slowly to begin, break down the technique. If you are not competent to do the technique / trick then have a player demonstrate it for you. Have each group stand opposite one another 10 to 20 yards apart with a ball each. They must move towards each other on a call (everyone in unison) and always move to the right or to the left as they get close to each other.

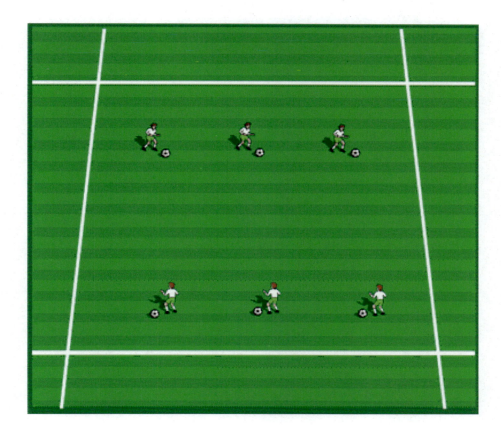

Warm up: Awareness Dribbling Work

Progression:

1. SEMI COMPETITIVE: Have each group stand opposite one another 10 to 20 yards apart with a ball each. They must move towards each other on a call (everyone in unison) and always both move to the right or both players move to the left as they get close to each other. Do it slowly to begin and build up the pace as they become competent.

2. Have them get the timing right where they get about a stride apart, just out of tackling distance but close enough to commit a defender in a game.

3. Once they get past each other they stop and turn and go again on the next call. Do many repetitions with this to have them practice in this semi-passive way.

4. This is a good way to get many players working on the same skill in a small area with lots of work on the ball. Focus on one skill at a time and spend time on it to keep improving the technique of each player.

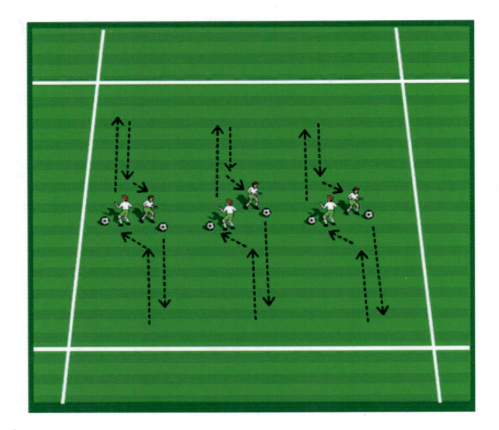

Groups play in 1 v 1 situations as above moving up and down the area practicing their moves.

Moves to work on here:

1. The Matthews
2. The Rivelino
3. The Scissors
4. The Double Touch

By practicing only four dribbles with the limited time we have it gives you a chance to improve each player in these techniques, it may be you only use two because of this. It is better to get good at a small number than practice many different ones and be good at none of them. I believe having up to three dribbles is enough for each player to use if they get very good at them.

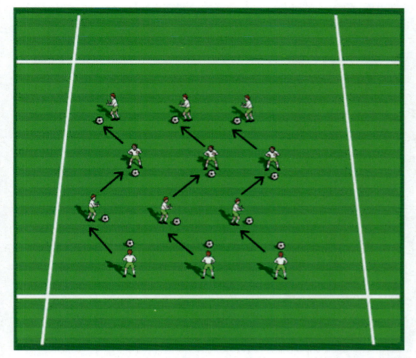

On the coaches command the players do a Matthews, Rivelino, double touch or Scissors (or their own ideas) to the left. They then stand still until the next command then do it to the right and so on. By doing it slowly it gives the players a chance to work and perfect the move. As they get competent the coach can get them to speed up the movement. Working up and down the field, right to left and left to right. This ensures they do it with both feet.

1. **The Matthews** – Big toe – little toe technique, lean one way, checks to the other. Bring the foot behind the ball to move it (for example, plant the left foot outside the ball to the left and bring the right inside the ball and move it away to the right with the right foot).
2. **The Rivelino** – Fake to kick the ball, step over the ball outside to inside then move the ball to the outside with the same foot (for example step over the ball with the right foot from right to left then take the ball away to the right with the right foot & accelerate away).
3. **The Scissors** – Step over the ball inside to outside then move the ball away with the other foot (for example, right foot inside to outside then move the ball to the left with the left foot).

You can also just fake them out with this by pretending to touch it the first time then touching it forward after the fake. Emphasize body position with this move, they need to have their body facing to the side they are pretending to move the ball also not keep it straight forward which is less likely to fool the defender. All techniques look to fake the opponent one way then move the ball the other way. On each dribble the player must drop their shoulder one way to move the other way.

ROUTINE:
1. Standing practicing the dribbling movement in a shadow style without touching the ball
2. Doing the movement on the spot with movement of the ball
3. Moving around freely in the area where it is congested; making the designated moves free style.

The Double Touch Dribble

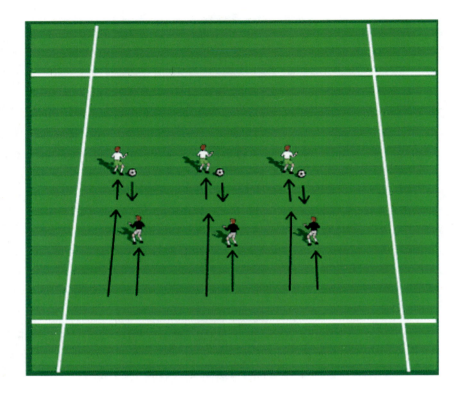

Double Touch (this is a great move to learn)

1. Running forward, bring the ball back with one touch then pass it forward to yourself with the second touch all the time keeping it in control at your feet. First touch back is to fake out the defender who is running alongside you, so they think you are stopping the ball or changing direction and they will check their forward run to react to this, but you continue to run forward by making the second touch forward and then get away from them. Rotate at the end of each run.

2. You can also just fake them out with this by pretending to touch it the first time then touching it forward after the fake.

3. Emphasize body position with this move, they need to have their body facing to the side they are pretending to move the ball also not keep it straight forward which is less likely to fool the defender.

4. All techniques look to fake the opponent one way then move the ball the other way. On each dribble the player must drop their shoulder one way to move the other way.

Ball Control and Dribbling Skills Ideas

He Says She Says

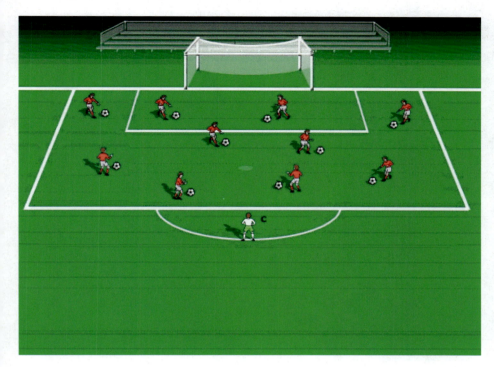

Emphasis: Ball control and motor skills

Set-up: Use the penalty box or the center circle. Grid size depends on the number of players. Each player has a ball.

Objective: The players must follow the instruction of the coach. For example, if the coach shouts "touch the ball quickly side to side", then the players must do so. Complete 10 commands successfully and then stretch for a minute. Repeat using different commands.

Progression:
1. Tap the top of the ball with the bottoms of your feet, alternating feet each time.
2. Jump over the ball.
3. Hop around the ball.
4. Skip around the ball.
5. Toss the ball up, hit it with your head, and catch it.
6. Use the bottom of your foot and move it in a circle.
7. Kick the ball in the air, turn, and catch it.

Coaching Points:
1. Get the touches right.
2. Don't run into anyone.

Indianapolis 500

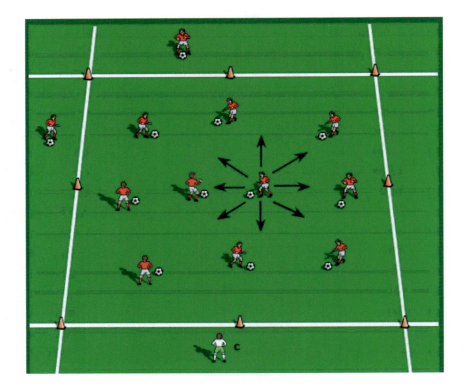

Emphasis: Dribbling, ball control

Set-up: Set up a 15x20 yard grid (race track). Place all of your players in the grid with a ball.

Objective: The players must not crash into the cones (rails). If the players (collide) with each other or the cones (rails), they must go outside the grid, and do fast footwork with the ball. For example; toe touches on the ball, quick passes side to side, or quick turns with the left and right foot. The players (cars) must obey the coaches (race director) shout. "Shift gears"-change directions, "red flag"-stop the ball, "blue flag"-stop the ball with the knee, "yellow flag"-dribble slower, and "green flag"-accelerate to top speed.

Progression:
1. Make the grid smaller and more congested.
2. Players must only use the left foot only.

Coaching Points:
1. Keep the ball close to your body.
2. Concentrate on change of direction away from pressure (other cars).

Change of Pace

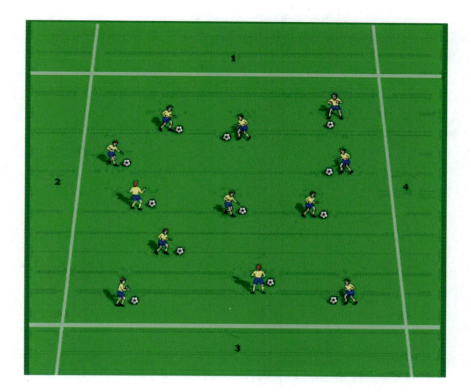

Emphasis: Dribbling

Set-up: 30 x 30 yard grid. 12-18 players start with a ball each inside the grid.

Objective: Each side of the grid is allocated a number – 1, 2, 3 or 4. Coach will shout commands that all players must follow. If coach shouts "1" all players must dribble to that side of the grid, if coach shouts "3" all players must dribble to that side of grid and so forth. Players must use all the surfaces of their feet to dribble as well as change direction on the coach's command.

Progression: Encourage players to dribble as fast as possible by making it a race situation.

Coaching Points:
1. Use as many surfaces of the foot as possible.
2. Do not "kick" ball; push it out in front of you.
3. Try to avoid collisions by keeping head up.

Set Them Free

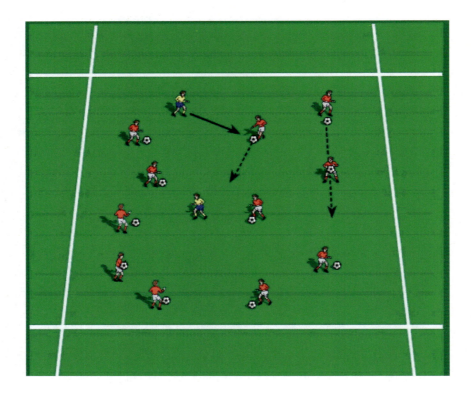

Emphasis: Dribbling for possession

Set-up: 20 x 20 yard grid. 12-18 players. Two sets of colored bibs.

Objective: 2 Players must wear colored bibs. On the coach's command these players pursue all other players who are dribbling freely inside the grid. If one of the "chasers" touches a player's ball then that player must freeze in that spot with the ball above their head and their legs apart. A player can only be "unfrozen" by another player dribbling a ball through their legs. After a designated time (approx 1min) count how many players are frozen? Allow all players to have a chance at being a chaser.

Progression: Increase the number of chasers.

Coaching Points:
1. Quick changes of direction and speed are essential to avoid "chasers"
2. Keep head up to detect oncoming opponents.
3. Encourage accelerations to escape from opponents.

Avoid The Defenders

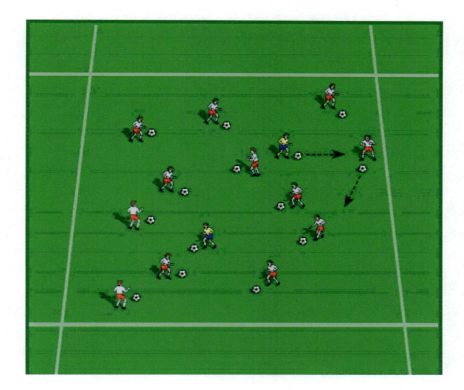

Emphasis: Dribbling for possession

Set-up: 20 x 20 yard grid. 12-18 players. Two sets of colored bibs. One ball for each player.

Objective: 2 players are identified as "chasers" by wearing a different colored bib. All players including the "chasers" must keep control of their ball at all times. If, while dribbling, a player is tagged by a "chaser" then that person must stay in one place and practice juggling the ball. Time is kept to see how long it takes for the two chasers to "stick" all the other players. Alternate chasers after each game.

Progression:
1. Increase the number of chasers.
2. Introduce a new feint or move to avoid opponents.

Coaching Points:
1. Quick changes of direction and speed are essential to avoid "chasers"
2. Keep head up to detect oncoming opponents.
3. Encourage the use of feints to escape from opponents.

Shadow Him

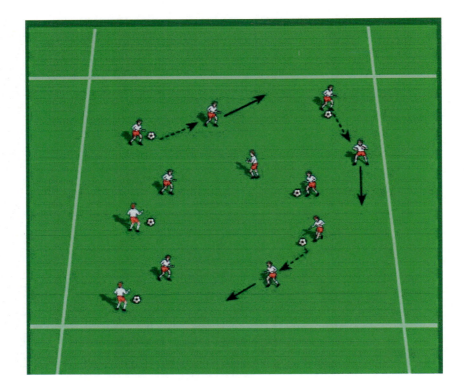

Emphasis: Dribbling

Set-up: 20 x 20 yard grid. 12-18 players. Players are in pairs with one ball.

Objective: Player 1 and 2 start approximately 2 yards apart, one behind the other. The player in the rear has the ball. Player in front must run around grid to try to lose his "shadow." Player with the ball is forced to dribble with close control and sped in order to keep up with his lead man. When coach shouts "switch" player with ball tries to pass ball through his partner's legs. At this point the roles are reversed.

Coaching Points:
1. Don't kick ball, push it out in front of you.
2. Keep head up to detect movements of partner
3. Use all surfaces of the feet while dribbling and turning.

Take A Chance

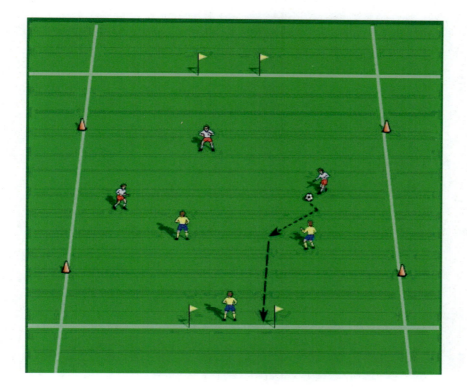

Emphasis: Dribbling for Possession and Penetration

Set-up: 20 x 30 yard grid with an area 4-5 yards wide designated as an end-zone (marked with cones). 6 players. Two sets of colored bibs. Flags to create mini goals at each end. Repeat set-up to accommodate entire team of 18 players.

Objective: A 3 v 3. One player is designated as a goalkeeper. Only the goalkeeper can use his hands in the end-zone. The goalkeeper must leave the end-zone to become an outfield player when his team is in possession of the ball. Players should try to dribble to create goal- scoring opportunities.

Progression: Award 3 points for a goal, 2 for beating an opponent and 1 for turning on an opponent.

Coaching Points:
1. Take defenders on!
2. Use feints, deception to elude defenders.

Objective: Emphasizing Dribbling Techniques with Fun Games

Emphasis: Dribbling

Set-up: 40 x 30 yard grid divided into 10 x 10 yard grids. Flags are placed to create a mini goal at one end of the grid. Two sets of colored bibs. Groups of 4-5 players.

Objective: One player starts in the middle 10 x 10 grid and will act as the defender. One player will act as a goalkeeper in the mini goal. The first player in line will attempt to dribble past the defender in the middle grid before attempting to score in the mini goal. A shot must be taken from greater than 10 yards from goal. The attacker then becomes the defender for the next attempt.

Progression:
1. Players must use a feint to beat the defender.
2. Players can attack in pairs to create a 2v1 situation.

Coaching Points:
1. Push ball out in front while moving at speed.
2. Accelerate over the first few yards to unsettle defender.
3. Use feints, deception to elude defenders.

Speed Dribble

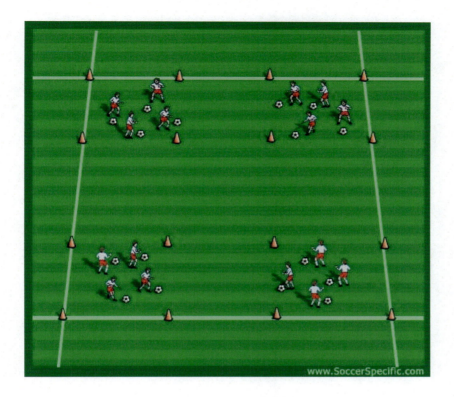

Emphasis: Dribbling

Set-up: 30 x 30 yard grid. Cones are placed to create corner areas of approximately 5 x 5 yards. 4-5 players in each corner. 1 ball per player.

Objective: On coaches' command "Switch" players must dribble at speed to a new corner area. To encourage speed dribbling, the first group to successfully arrive in a new corner wins the game.

Progression:
1. Players must juggle 5 times in the new corner before the game can end.
2. Add defenders (2-3) in centre if grid to try to steal balls from players.

Coaching Points:
1. Push ball out in front while moving at speed.
2. Keep head and eyes up to avoid collisions.
3. Use feints, deception to elude defenders.

Turn and Dribble

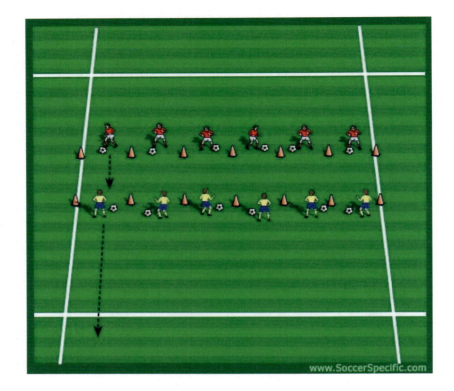

Emphasis: Running with the ball at speed, change of speed.

Set-up: 30 x 30 yard grid. 12-18 players with a ball each. Two sets of colored bibs. Players arranged in pairs facing each other. Cones placed to create a 5-yard wide channel between each pair. All players are performing fast footwork type activities in a stationary space.

Objective: Coach calls out the color of one of the teams. Example "Reds", at this time the red team must dribble quickly towards their opposite yellow partner. The objective is to tag the yellow player before they can turn and dribble over the end-line.

Progression: The team of chasers must try to pass their balls against the legs of their opponents.

Coaching Points:
1. Accelerate quickly in the direction you want to go.
2. Take longer touches; don't get the ball caught under your feet.

Moving Targets

Emphasis: Passing and Dribbling

Objective: 2 players are designated as "destroyers". The "destroyers" dribble around grid trying to pass their ball against another ball or legs of an opponent. If a player's ball or legs are struck then he too becomes a "destroyer". The last player to get struck by a "destroyer" is the winner.

Progression: Destroyers can strike their opponents ball only.

Coaching Points:
1. Keep head and eyes up to avoid opponents as well as locate targets.
2. Changes of speed to get close to opponent prior to passing ball.

Objective: Improving Players Dribbling Skills Ability in a 1 v 1

Emphasis: Dribbling to beat an opponent, making positive forward runs with the ball.

Warm-up: 10 minutes – One ball per player. Unrestricted movement incorporating running, jogging, juggling and stretching Players move freely and getting comfortable on the ball. See Diagram below.

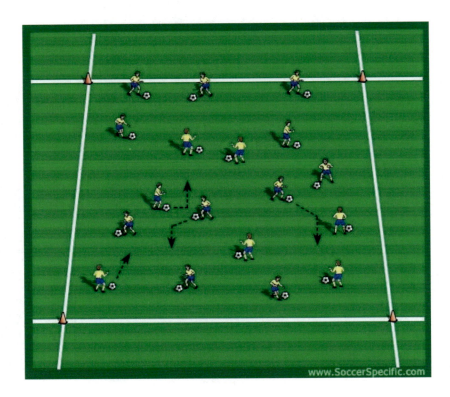

5 minutes – Unrestricted movement with an emphasis on various dribbling moves:

- Use outside of foot to push ball out of feet,
- Change of pace,
- Change of direction,
- Use disguise then change of pace and direction,
- Stress drop left shoulder, move body weight left, then push ball with outside of right foot – accelerate,
- Use a scissors movement with outside of left foot going around outside of ball – take with outside of right foot.

Exercise #1

Set-up: 10 x 30 yard grid divided into three 10 x 10 yard grids as shown in Diagram below. A halfway line is marked with flags at opposite sides of the grid. Three players per grid. Set-up is repeated to accommodate the entire squad of 18 players.

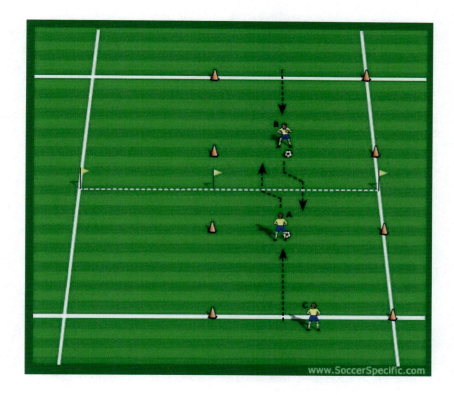

Objective: 5 minutes - Players (A) and (B) dribble towards the center line as illustrated above. Each player performs a feint at the halfway line before accelerating to the opposite side of the grid. (Ex) drop right shoulder, accelerate left. Sequence is repeated with all three players alternating.

Progression 1

5 minutes - Player (A) dribbles to the halfway line before passing to (B) as shown in below. Player (A) then moves forward to act as a passive defender. Player (B) performs a move and accelerates past the passive defender. The sequence is repeated with (B) passing the next ball to player (C) from the halfway line. Sequence is continuous for designated period of time.

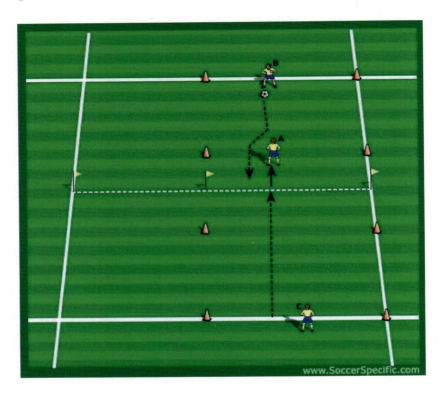

Progression 2

5 minutes - Player (A) dribbles to the halfway line and passes to (B) as shown in diagram below. As soon as player (B) has received the ball player (A) must move forward to defend. Player (A) can only defend in front of the cones marked (H). This will encourage (B) to attack at pace before the defender can get ready. Player (B) attempts to beat the defender and dribble towards the halfway line. Sequence is repeated in the opposite direction with (B) passing to (C) from the halfway line. Play is continuous for a designated period of time.

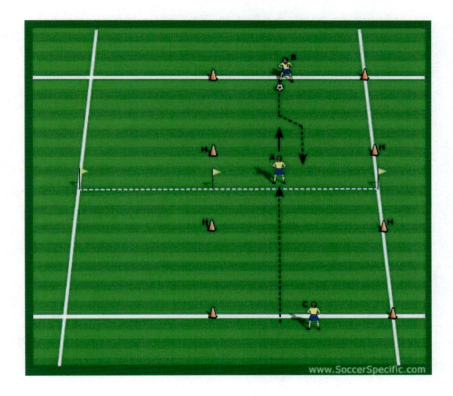

Progression 3

5 minutes - Player (A) starts on the halfway line. Players (B) and (C) are positioned at opposite ends of the grid as shown below. Player (B) passes to (A). Player (A) must make a choice: 1) Run at player (B) and dribble over the end line, 2) Turn and run at player (C) and dribble over the opposite end line. Players continuously rotate to become the middle player. The Diagram below illustrates player (A) turning to run at defender (C).

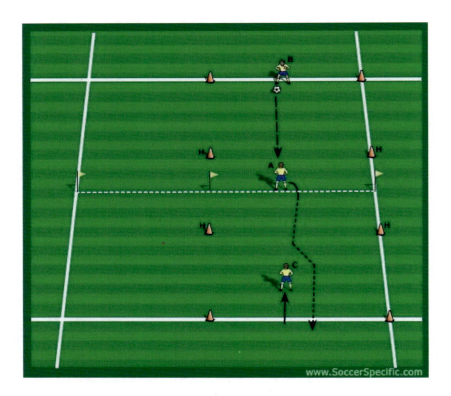

Exercise #2

Set-up: 20 x 30 yard grid as shown in the diagram below. A 3 v 3 is organized in the playing area. Set-up is repeated to accommodate the entire squad.

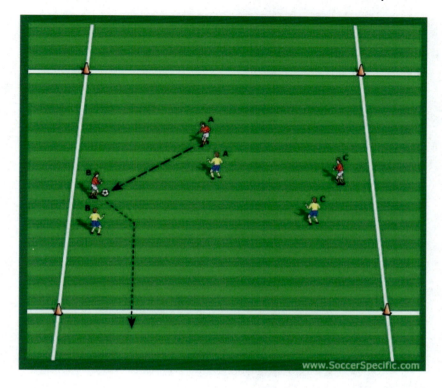

Objective: 5 minutes - Players are paired off as shown in Diagram (f) above. Red (A) must play against Yellow (A), Red (B) must play against Yellow (B) and so forth. Since each player has a direct opponent, if a player beats his opponent he should have a direct run to score. Players score by dribbling over their opponents' end line.

Coaching Points:
1. Spread end to end to create space.
2. When your team is in possession, create 1v1 situations by moving away from the player on the ball.
3. Think dribble, be positive.
4. Attack at pace.
5. Use disguise.

Progression (1): 5 minutes - The team that scores maintains possession and attacks in the opposite direction. This creates a greater incentive to continue to score.

Progression (2): 5 minutes - Eliminate the direct opponent assignment. Players are no longer required to only stay with their man.

Dribbling to Beat an Opponent Making Positive Forward Runs with The Ball

Warm-up: 10 minutes – One ball per player. Unrestricted movement incorporating running, jogging, juggling and stretching. Players move freely getting comfortable on the ball.

Use outside of foot to push ball out of feet. Change of pace and change of direction. Use disguise then change of pace and direction,

Stress drop left shoulder, move body weight left, then push ball with outside of right foot – accelerate. Use a scissors movement with outside of left foot going around outside of ball – take with outside of right foot.

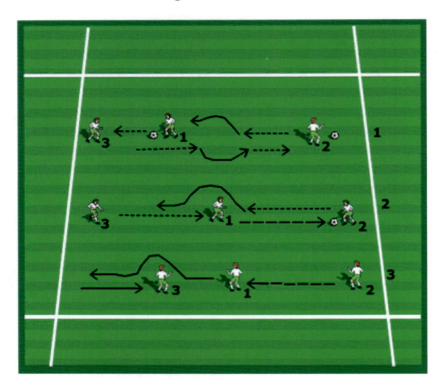

Exercise 1:

Setup: 10 x 30 yard grid divided into three 10 x 10 yard grids. A halfway line is marked with flags at opposite sides of the grid. Three players per grid. Set-up is repeated to accommodate the entire squad.

Objective: 5 minutes - Players (1) and (2) dribble towards the center line. Each player performs a feint at the halfway line before accelerating to the opposite side of the grid. (Ex) drop right shoulder, accelerate left. Sequence is repeated with all three players alternating.

Progression (1): 5 minutes - Player (1) dribbles to the halfway line before passing to (2). Player (1) then moves forward to act as a passive defender. Player (2) performs a move and accelerates past the passive defender. The sequence is repeated with (2) passing the next ball to player (3) from near the halfway line. Sequence is continuous for designated period of time.

Progression (2): 5 minutes - Player (1) dribbles to the halfway line and passes to (2.) As soon as player (2) has received the ball player (1) must move forward to defend. Player (1) can only defend in front of the cones. This will encourage (2) to attack at pace before the defender can get ready. Player (2) attempts to beat the defender and dribble towards the halfway line. Sequence is repeated in the opposite direction with (2) passing to (3) from the halfway line. Play is continuous for a designated period of time.

Progression (3): 5 minutes - Player (1) starts on the halfway line. Players (2) and (3) are positioned at opposite ends of the grid. Player (2) passes to (1). Player (1) must make a choice: a) Run at player (2) and dribble over the end line, b) Turn and run at player (3) and dribble over the opposite end line. Players continuously rotate to become the middle player. Here player (1) turns to run at defender (3).

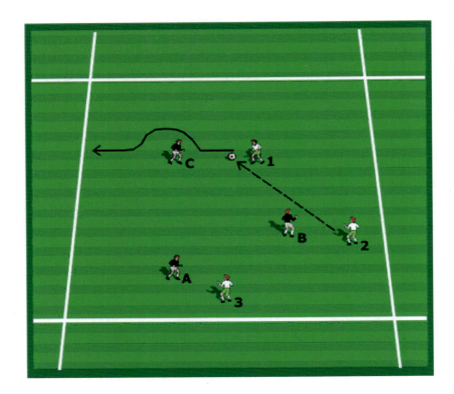

Exercise 2:

Setup: 20 x 30 yard grid as shown above. A 3 v 3 is organized in the playing area. Set-up is repeated to accommodate the entire squad.

Objective: 5 minutes - Players are paired off. (1) Must play against (C), (2) must play against (B) and so forth. Since each player has a direct opponent, if a player beats his opponent he should have a direct run to score. Players score by dribbling over their opponents' end line.

Coaching Points:
1. Spread end to end to create space.
2. When your team is in possession, create 1 v 1 situations by moving away from the player on the ball.
3. Think dribble, be positive.
4. Attack at pace.
5. Use disguise

Progression (1): 5 minutes - The team that scores maintains possession and attacks in the opposite direction. This creates a greater incentive to continue to score.

Progression (2): 5 minutes - Eliminate the direct opponent assignment. Players are no longer required to only stay with their man.

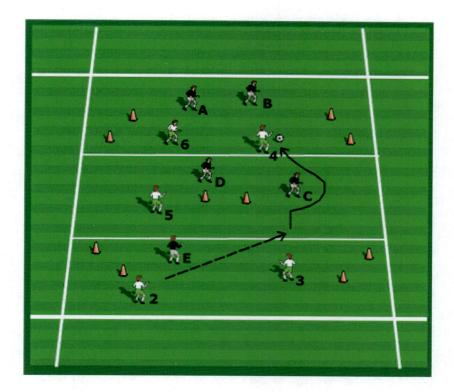

Exercise 3:

Objective: 15 minutes - Both teams compete for possession of the ball. Players are positioned in each of the thirds of the field as shown. Players score by dribbling over the opponents' end line or by dribbling through any of the five gates located in the playing area. Players can only leave their third of the field by dribbling forward. Here player (4) receiving a pass, beating his marker and dribbling into the next third of the field.

Coaching Points:
1. Encourage dribbling in all areas.
2. Spread out side-to-side and end-to-end.
3. Spread immediately when goalkeeper receives the ball.
4. Attack at pace.
5. Create 1 v 1 situations by moving away from the player in possession.

Dribbling Skills

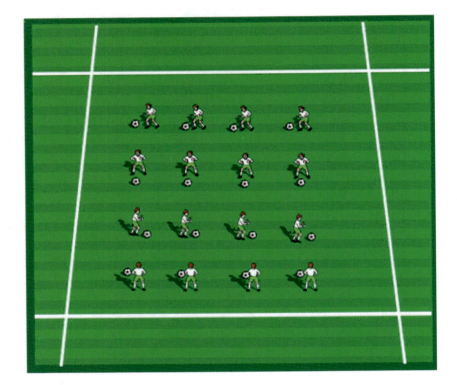

1. The above set up is an example of the progressive movement of one group of players. You can have 4 groups set up this way.

2. Practicing a dribble from bottom to top, this is the routine working around the ball four times on the call of the coach each time facing another 45 degrees around the ball. Make the move then stop and wait for the next call. All players work in unison.

3. This is the total movement of one line of players but work with two lines opposite each other to help the development of the session (see over). Move around the ball both ways so players work on both sides with both feet. You get four dribbles / moves per rotation. Do it slowly to begin, break down the technique. If the coach is not competent to do the technique / trick him or herself, have a player demonstrate it.

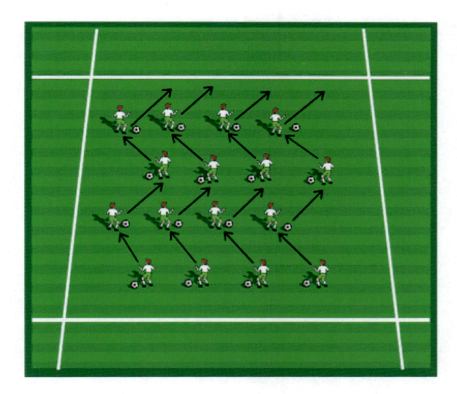

1. On the coaches command the players do a Matthews, Rivelino or Scissors to the left. They then stand still until the next command then do it to the right and so on. By doing it slowly it gives the players a chance to work and perfect the move. As they get competent the coach can get them to speed up the movement. Working up and down the field, right to left and left to right. This ensures they do it with both feet.

2. The Matthews – Big toe – little toe technique, lean one way, check to the other. Bring the foot behind the ball to move it (for example, plant the left foot outside the ball to the left and bring the right inside the ball and move it away to the right with the right foot).

3. The Rivelino – Fake to kick the ball, step over the ball outside to inside then move the ball to the outside with the same foot (for example step over the ball with the right foot from right to left then take the ball away to the right with the right foot and accelerate away).

4. The Scissors – Step over the ball inside to outside then move the ball away with the other foot (for example, right foot inside to outside then move the ball to the left with the left foot).

Double Touch Movement

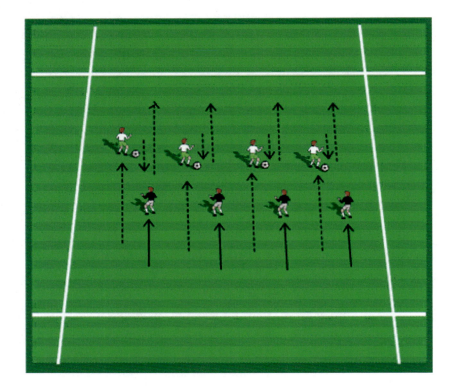

1. Double Touch - Running forward, bring the ball back with one touch then pass it forward to yourself with the second touch all the time keeping it in control at your feet. First touch back is to fake out the defender who is running alongside you, so they think you are stopping the ball or changing direction and they will check their forward run to react to this, but you continue to run forward by making the second touch forward and then get away from them. Rotate at the end of each run.

2. You can also just fake them out with this by pretending to touch it the first time then touching it forward after the fake.

3. Emphasize body position with this move, they need to have their body facing to the side they are pretending to move the ball also not keep it straight forward which is less likely to fool the defender. All techniques look to fake the opponent one way then move the ball the other way. On each dribble the player must drop their shoulder one way to move the other way.

Dribbling Set Up

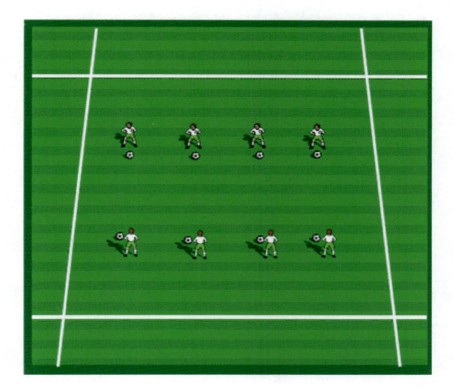

1. Develop – Have each group stand opposite one another 10 to 20 yards apart with a ball each. They must move towards each other on a call (everyone in unison) and always move to the right or to the left as they get close to each other. Do it slowly to begin and build up the pace as they become competent.

2. Have them get the timing right where they get about a stride apart, just out of tackling distance but close enough to commit a defender in a game.

3. Once they get past each other they stop and turn and go again on the next call. Do many repetitions with this to have them practice in this semi-passive way.

4. This is a good way to get many players working on the same skill in a small area with lots of work on the ball. Focus on one skill at a time and spend time on it to keep improving the technique of each player.

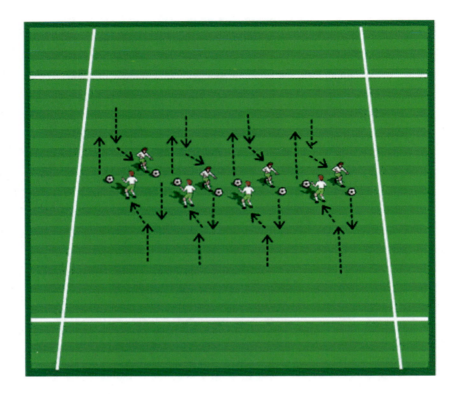

Groups play in 1 v 1 situations as above moving up and down the area practicing their moves. Moves to work on here are:

1. The Matthews.
2. The Rivelino.
3. The Scissors.

By practicing only three dribbles with the limited time we have it gives you a chance to improve each player in these techniques, it may be you only use two because of this. It is better to get good at a small number than practice many different ones and be good at none of them. I believe having up to three dribbles is enough for each player to use if they get very good at them.

Using Dribbling Games to Improve Individual Dribbling Skills

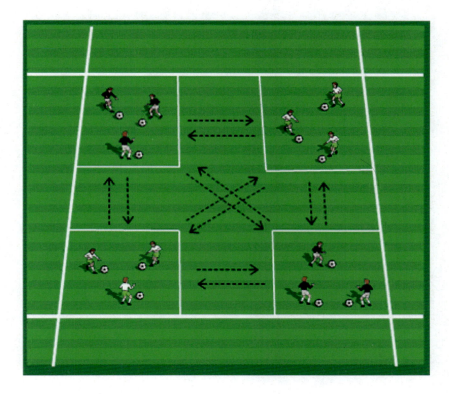

Have a ball for each player. Split into four groups dribbling in their own grid practicing designated dribbling moves and turns. On the command of the coach they dribble as fast as they can to another grid avoiding other players by dribbling through them. Make it competitive by having the first three players in a grid with their foot on the ball as the winners.

Coach stands in the middle, 3 go at once and cut to the next group continue dribbling in that group till it's their turn again. Coach can determine the cut with the outside of the foot, inside of the foot, full turn away from pressure (inside or outside of foot), Dummy step over, drag back and turn (ball behind other foot), step over and take. Rotate so they go both ways.

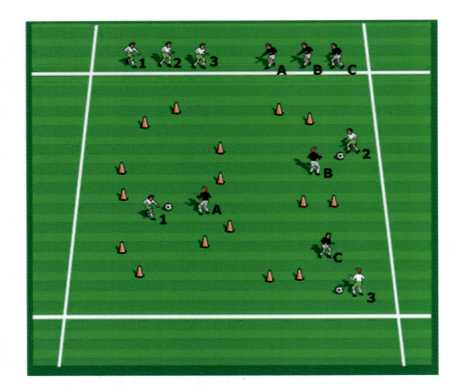

One team a ball each, the other team players try to win a ball and keep it. A player can win any ball off any of the other team's players. Once a player has lost the ball they have to try to win one back off another player. After a time period see which team has the most soccer balls. This is very competitive and the players get a chance to practice dribbling and running with the ball, shielding the ball from defenders.

FOCUS ON THE MATTHEWS, SCISSORS; RIVELINO AND DOUBLE TOUCH DRIBBLES FROM THE PREVIOUS WEEKS (OR YOUR OWN IDEAS).

Shadow Dribbling Games

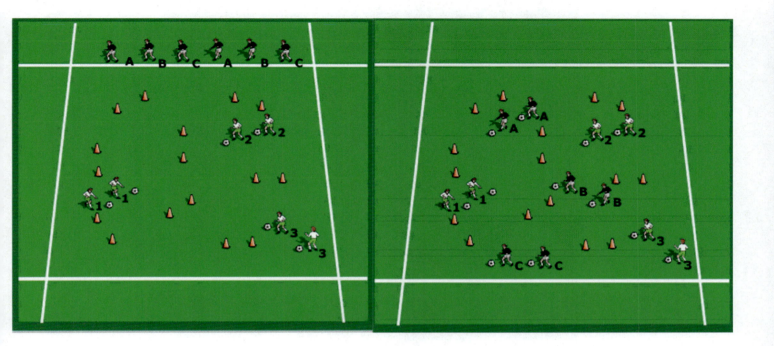

1. Players in pairs, a ball each one has to shadow the other making the same movements. Lead players try to lose their shadows that must try and touch the leader. Rotate positions.

2. Movements include dribbling with the outside of the foot only, the inside only, left foot / right foot only, turn and face your shadow and dummy them etc.

3. Have the lead player face up to their shadow and throw a feint to get away again.

4. Try all players in at once to cause congestion so players need to watch their leader but also be aware of where other players are (improves peripheral vision).

5. Introduce the kick out game for some fun; keep possession of your own ball kick someone else's out the area. Make it free so you can kick anyone's ball out, the players are working for themselves. Have three chances each player, once out three times then the outside players must juggle with the ball to keep involved in some practice.

1 v 1

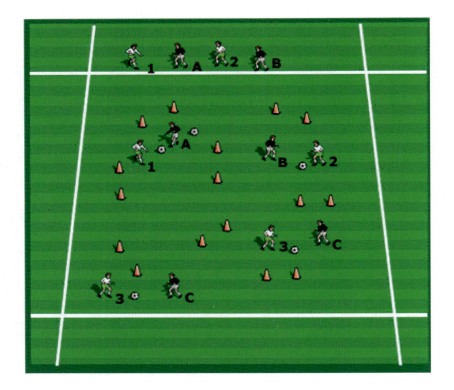

1 v 1's with eight goals to score in. This is an intensive workout where each player must try to keep possession of the ball and at the same time score by dribbling through a goal. They work for two minutes and count the number of goals they score through the various goals.

Each player tries to gain possession of the ball. Once their time is up they get a chance to recover whilst the other group goes.

2 v 2

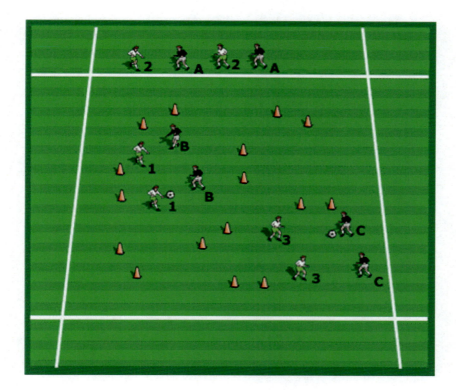

Two games of two v two played at the same time. (1)'s play against (B)'s and (3)'s play against (C)'s. Rotate. (2)'s then play against (A)'s whilst the first 2 groups have a rest.

Same idea scoring through the goals but players can pass through them to their teammate and that counts as a goal as well as dribbling through them.

Introducing passing, support play, switching play, 1 – 2's, crossovers etc as well as when and where to dribble.

Build up to two 3 v 3 games then finish with a possession game with eight goals to score in playing 6 v 6.

1 v 1 Attacking Confrontations

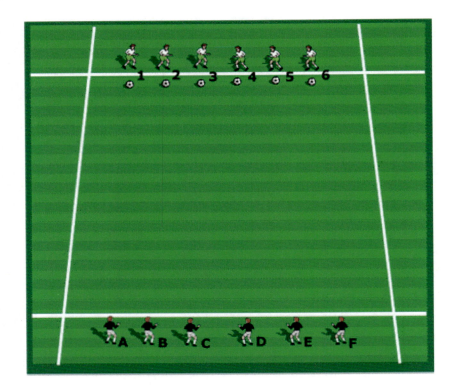

This set up creates lots of opportunities of 1 v 1 confrontations with different players against each other. Begin with players passing and defending passively so the player on the ball dribbles past the defender successfully.

Each numbered player has a ball and they can pass to any lettered player. They call their name, pass the ball and close them down quickly and the lettered player has to beat them and score a goal by stopping the ball anywhere along the line where the numbered players begin. If the numbered player wins back the ball they score by stopping the ball on the lettered player's line. This is a big area to be able to score on which improves the chances of success. Have at least three 1 v 1 's going at any one time, players dictate when and where they do this depending on how many others are live in their 1 v 1's. Players need to be aware of the positions of the other 1 v 1 confrontations so they do not clash with them. Ensure all players have the opportunity to be the attacking player in the 1 v 1.

Competitive: Each player counts the number of goals they score, use this on an individual and team basis so there is a winning team and ultimately a winning player.

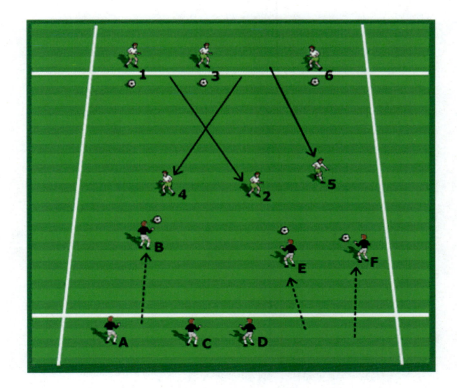

This shows the set up and how the game works with 6 players involved with 1 v 1's at any one time.

Players can use all the area to beat each other.

A Game Situation for 1 v 1's

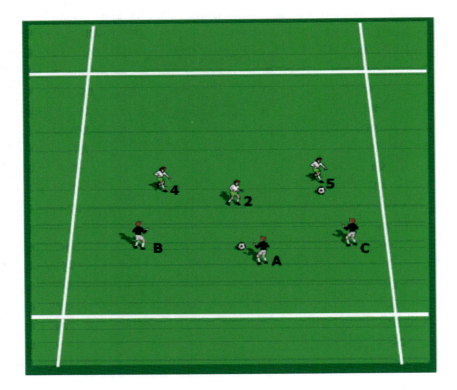

Divide the teams up into two 3 v 3 games with teams attacking the long side lines to score a goal. Play with one ball then two balls so there is some 1 v 1's and also some support play. Then they attack the short sides as targets making it a little harder to succeed.

ABOUT WAYNE HARRISON

Married to Mary for 30 years with two daughters Sophie 26 and Johanna 23.

Wayne is available for Soccer Symposiums and Conventions wherever they are needed; and able to offer field clinics and classroom presentations of your choosing. He has vast experience in this field of work.

His specialist system of play is the 4-2-3-1. His favored type of development training is that of creating the "THINKING PLAYER" through his SOCCER AWARENESS methods of coaching.

His belief is developing the MIND of the player through ONE TOUCH training, which is purely to help the development of the SKILL FACTOR (the when, where how and why of decision making; or the thinking process). He wants all coaches to teach where it is the player who becomes the decision maker not the coach.

You can contact him on soccerawareness@outlook.com and / or view his website www.soccerawareness.com.

This book was reproduced in partnership with Amplified Soccer Marketing, LLC. Find out more at www.amplifiedsoccer.com.

GET THESE ADDITIONAL BOOKS AT WWW.SOCCERAWARENESS.COM

Soccer Awareness Training
Tactical Thoughts on the Development of the New 4 v 4, 7 v 7 and 9 v 9 Game Sizes

eBook 25
How to Play the 4-2-3-1: Attacking and Defensive Positioning

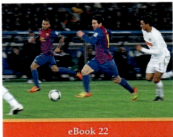
eBook 22
Quick Break and Counter Attacking Development Plan

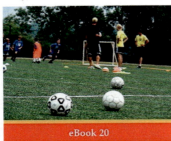
eBook 20
Connecting Small Sided Games with 8 v 8 and 11 v 11

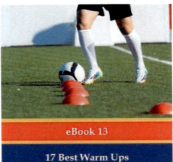
eBook 13
17 Best Warm Ups

eBook 12
16 Team Shape Games Based On Age Group Sizes Of Games

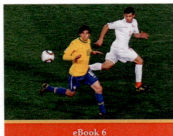
eBook 6
Sideways On or Facing Forward Body Shape for Striker Position; The Brazilian Way

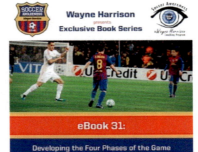
eBook 31:
Developing the Four Phases of the Game

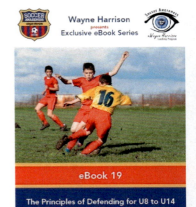
eBook 19
The Principles of Defending for U8 to U14

GET THESE ADDITIONAL BOOKS AT
WWW.SOCCERAWARENESS.COM

eBook 18
Identifying and Solving Common Game Situation Problems in the Training Environment

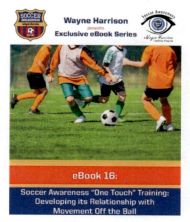

eBook 16:
Soccer Awareness "One Touch" Training: Developing its Relationship with Movement Off the Ball

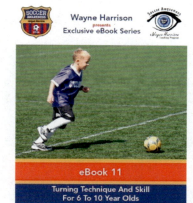

eBook 11
Turning Technique And Skill For 6 To 10 Year Olds

eBook 8:
Small-Sided Games for Strikers

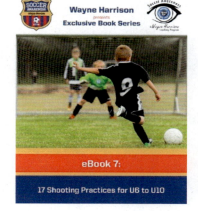

eBook 7:
17 Shooting Practices for U6 to U10

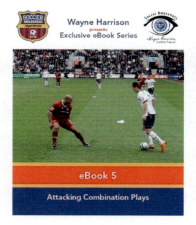

eBook 5
Attacking Combination Plays

eBook 4
Attacking and Defending Games: Challenging the Mindset and Mental Transition of the Players

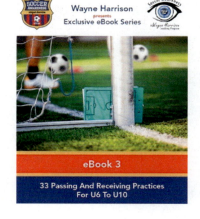

eBook 3
33 Passing And Receiving Practices For U6 To U10

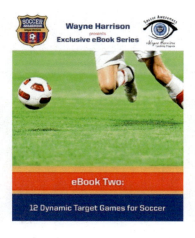

eBook Two:
12 Dynamic Target Games for Soccer

Made in the USA
Middletown, DE
23 November 2016